Your Amazing Skin from Outside In

Your Amazing Skin from Outside In

by Joanne Settel, PhD

illustrated by Bonnie Timmons

Atheneum Books for Young Readers

atheneum   New York London Toronto Sydney New Delhi

atheneum

ATHENEUM BOOKS FOR YOUNG READERS

An imprint of Simon & Schuster Children's Publishing Division

1230 Avenue of the Americas, New York, New York 10020

Text copyright © 2018 by Joanne Settel

Illustrations copyright © 2018 by Bonnie Timmons

Special thanks to Dr. Oluwatobi Ogbechie-Godec, MD MBA, resident physician at NYU Dermatology, for sharing her expertise and input.

ATHENEUM BOOKS FOR YOUNG READERS is a registered trademark of Simon & Schuster, Inc.

Atheneum logo is a trademark of Simon & Schuster, Inc.

For information about special discounts for bulk purchases, please contact Simon & Schuster Special Sales at 1-866-506-1949 or business@simonandschuster.com.

The Simon & Schuster Speakers Bureau can bring authors to your live event. For more information or to book an event, contact the Simon & Schuster Speakers Bureau at 1-866-248-3049 or visit our website at www.simonspeakers.com.

Book design by Debra Sfetsios-Conover

The text for this book was set in Archer Book.

The illustrations for this book were rendered digitally on an iPad Pro and a Mac desktop.

Manufactured in China

0718 SCP

First Edition

10 9 8 7 6 5 4 3 2 1

Library of Congress Cataloging-in-Publication Data

Names: Settel, Joanne, author. | Timmons, Bonnie, illustrator.

Title: Your amazing skin from outside in / Joanne Settel, Ph.D. ; illustrated by Bonnie Timmons.

Description: First edition. | New York : Atheneum Books for Young Readers, [2018] | Audience: Ages 8 up. | Audience: Grades 3 up. | Includes bibliographical references and index.

Identifiers: LCCN 2014017401 | ISBN 9781481422055 (hardcover) | ISBN 9781481422062 (eBook)

Subjects: LCSH: Skin—Juvenile literature. | Skin—Juvenile poetry. |Children's questions and answers.

Classification: LCC QM484 .S48 2018 | DDC 612.7/9—dc23

LC record available at https://lccn.loc.gov/2014017401

To Barry, who is my rock.
And to Mikaela and Braydon,
who are my inspiration.
—J. S.

For my beautiful,
red-haired sister, Jan,
who has defeated melanoma
and who doggedly stays in
the shade
—B. T.

CONTENTS

PART I

What's in This Skin? The Basics — 1

You Won't Believe What Skin Can Do — 2

Layers and Layers and Layers of Skin — 4

PART II

Blushing, Tanning, Freckled Skin — 9

Black, Brown, White, and Pinkish Skin — 10

Some Kids Tan and Some Kids Burn — 14

Freckles, Freckles Everywhere — 18

When I'm Embarrassed I Turn Red — 21

My Fingers Get White in the Snow — 22

PART III

Sweaty, Bumpy, Wrinkly Skin — 24

My Fingerprints Give Me Away — 25

I've Got Blue Ink All Over Me — 28

My Fingers Wrinkle in the Pool — 29

Goose Bumps Popped Up on My Skin — 31

Sweaty, Sweaty Me — 35

We're Getting Stinky — 38

PART IV

Cut, Bruised, Scabby Skin — 41

I Cut My Thumb — 42

Black and Blue and Yellow, Too — 45

I've Got a Scab I Want to Pick — 49

PART V

Itchy, Sizzling, Peeling Skin — 50

Mosquitoes Love Me! — 51

I'm So Itchy — 54

Ouch! I've Got a Sunburn — 56

I'm Losing My Skin!   59

My Skin Is Hot, But I Feel Cold   61

PART VI

Pimply, Blistered, Warty Skin   64

I've Got a Pimple on My Nose   65

I've Got a Blister on My Toe   69

I Hate This Wart   72

CONCLUSION

Your Skin Will Thank You, That's for Sure!   75

Glossary   77

*(Note: first appearance of glossary words appear in bold in the text.)

For More Information   81

     Useful Websites   81

     References and Additional Reading   82

Index   87

PART I
WHAT'S IN THIS SKIN? THE BASICS

It peels, it heals, it itches, too.
It warms you, cools you, turns you blue.
I'll show you how, and when we're through,
you won't believe what skin can do!

And that's not all: we'll peek inside
where different kinds of skin cells hide
and find out how each tiny cell
allows your skin to work so well.

You Won't Believe What Skin Can Do

Skin covers you, now that's for sure.
But really, skin does much, much more.
One thing it does is keep stuff out,
like germs, and bugs that lurk about.

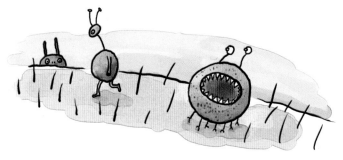

But here's a funny thing: your skin
will also let some stuff get *in*,
like sunlight's **UV rays**, and heat,
which warms you up from head to feet.

Plus, using sunlight's energy,
skin makes a **vitamin** called **D**:
a **nutrient** that scientists know
will help our bones get thick and grow.

Another way skin's really great
is it can **thermoregulate**.

So summer, winter, spring, and fall
your temperature won't change at all.

When you are hot, your skin makes sweat
'cause skin will cool when it gets wet.
And when you're cold, your coat of skin
will help to hold your warmth within.

And one more thing! In skin, one finds
the sensing cells: so many kinds!
Cells on the top and deep within
sense all the things you feel with skin.

Some help detect what's smooth or rough,
some if your room is warm enough,
some pick up tickles, some a touch,
some feel those shoes that pinch too much.

So clearly, it's the job of skin
to keep things out and let things in.
To keep you warm or cool you down
and let you sense what's all around.

COOL FACTS ABOUT SKIN

- If you could measure all your skin, you'd be surprised to learn how much there is. Our skin is the largest **organ** in the body. An adult man has around nineteen to twenty square feet of skin. This is almost the size of the door to your bedroom (twenty-one square feet)!

- Some animals can use their skin to breathe. Frogs, for example, have lungs, but they get most of their **oxygen** through their very thin skin. Eels can breathe through their skin when they move around on land. (When not on land, they use gills to get oxygen from the water.) Earthworms are the real skin breathers: They get all their oxygen this way.

  Skin-breathing animals can lose a lot of water through their thin skins, so they must live in damp areas. Human skin is too thick for skin breathing, but the thickness helps keep water inside. Since people are made of more than 50 percent water, it's important that we don't lose too much of it to the air.

- Young caecilians eat their mother's skin. Caecilians are legless amphibians that look like big earthworms, but they are actually related to frogs and salamanders. Caecilian moms grow extra-thick skin for their young to feed on. Yum!

Layers and Layers and Layers of Skin

To understand our skin, we'll start
by looking at each separate part.
An **epidermis**, which can grow,
and then the **dermis**, deep below.

The epidermis is a wall
of cells, some forty layers tall.
On top, the cells are dead and dying;
deeper down, they're multiplying.

The bottom **cells divide** nonstop
and push into the cells on top,
which, by the thousands, then are **shed**
into the air, the bath and bed.

These cells are tiny, small, and thin.
You'll never see them leave your skin.
But actually, they're everywhere.
They make the dust that fills the air.

They make the dust that fills the air.

Each day, you're making thousands more,
and these replace those lost before,
so that your epidermal wall
is always forty layers tall.

The epidermis needs a base
to hold its stack of cells in place.
This is the dermis, right below
those epidermal cells that grow.

Inside the dermis of the skin
are protein threads called **collagen**,
which coil like springs, so skin can then
be stretched and still spring back again.

What's more, the dermis of our skin
has **capillary** tubes within.
These carry blood, which will provide
the stuff skin needs to stay alive.

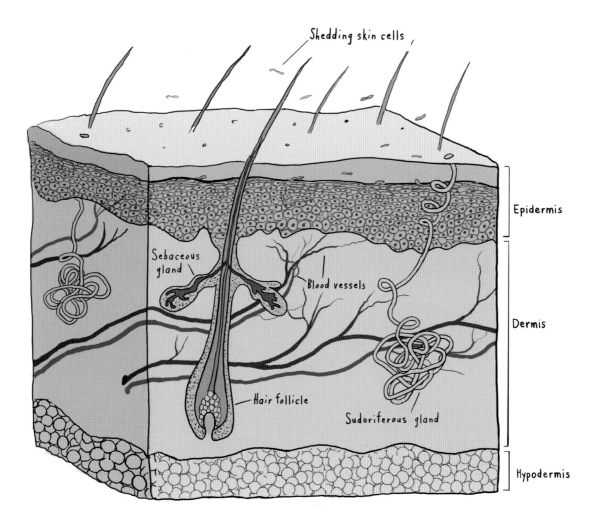

Shedding skin cells

Epidermis

Sebaceous
gland

Blood vessels

Dermis

Hair follicle

Sudoriferous gland

Hypodermis

Up from these blood tubes, things **diffuse**,
like nutrients that skin cells use.
Both oxygen and sugars go
into your cells, so they can grow.

The dermal layer's also got
receptors that can sense it's hot,
and lots of other **sensors**, such
as those for cold and pain and touch.

And through the dermis, everywhere,
are **follicles** that hold our hair.
To oil the hairs, each tiny strand
has one big, round **sebaceous gland**.

But that's not all! We're not done yet.
Our skin has glands that make us sweat.
These **sudoriferous glands** are what
help cool us down when we get hot.

Below the skin, spread all around,
the **hypodermis** can be found.
It's where our yellow fat cells hide
to hold our body's heat inside.

So all in all, our skin's got two
main parts, both with key jobs to do.
The epidermis that protects,
and deeper dermis that comes next.

COOL FACTS ABOUT LAYERS OF SKIN

- Most of our skin is around two millimeters thick, about the thickness of a nickel. Our palms and soles have much thicker skin: around four millimeters, or two nickels' worth.

- Rhinoceroses have the thickest skin in the animal kingdom. In some parts of a rhino's body, its skin can be 35 millimeters, or around 1.3 inches, thick. That's a little more than seventeen stacked nickels in thickness! Thick skin protects these animals from the sharp claws of predators and the horns of other rhinos when they fight.

- You can easily see for yourself what fat looks like. Peel the skin off an uncooked chicken from the grocery store, and you will see that just below it is a layer of fat. This layer is the chicken's hypodermis, and it is not actually part of the skin; it is loosely attached to the skin's dermis. Our hypodermis is just like a chicken's.

    (Be sure to wash your hands carefully with soap and water anytime you touch raw chicken. Raw chicken sometimes carries salmonella bacteria that can make you sick.)

PART II
BLUSHING, TANNING, FRECKLED SKIN

Our different skins come in a range
of colors that can sometimes change.
Emotions, sun, and cold snow might
make skin turn red or tan or white.

So, in this section, we'll begin
to look at all the shades of skin
and see why skin can change and then
go back to what it was again.

Black, Brown, White, and Pinkish Skin

My friends all come in different shades.
One's darkish brown, another's beige.
One's very pale, a mix, I think
of lots of white and bits of pink.

And it is very strange to me
that when we flip our hands, we see
some pink and orange shades, but not
the color that we see on top.

Oh, Dr. Jo, please fill me in
on all the different shades of skin,
and why some kids have hands that show
dark shades on top and pinks below.

These browns and pinks and darks and lights
come from cells called **melanocytes**.
Melanocytes are tightly packed
within the epidermal stack.

It's there they work, deep in our skin,
to make some stuff called **melanin**.
This melanin spreads all around
to other skin cells, up and down.

We make most of our melanin
in places where the sun gets in—
so less on palms and soles of feet,
where sun and skin don't often meet.

Plus, when the sun *does* hit these spots,
they're more protected: they've got lots
of extra layers. Thicker skin
won't let those harmful sun rays in.

Two types of melanin are found:
one yellow-red, one blackish-brown.
And the amount of each that's made
is what gives you your special shade.

So, if you're darker, it's been found
that you produce more blackish-brown,
but if you're pale, with redder hair,
you've got more yellow-red stuff there.

Why reds and browns, but never greens?
It's all been coded in your **genes**!
Your genes tell each melanocyte
to make you dark or make you light.

Another thing that will affect
all of those skin shades you detect
is blood, which flows deep in our skin
and brings red **hemoglobin** in.

The blood will make some red show through
and give light skins a pinkish hue.
But if you're dark, then that will mean
that pinks and reds cannot be seen.

Then finally, the last of all—
although its presence can be small—
some orange-yellow (never green)
comes from the **pigment carotene**.

This carotene gets into you
from food like carrots; spinach, too.
And then your blood absorbs it in,
where it can seep into your skin.

Now, carotene will only show
in spots where melanins are low.
So, often palms and soles alone
are where you'll see an orange tone.

So, blood can add a reddish hue,
while orange carotene peeks through,
but mostly it's melanocytes
that give your skin its darks and lights.

COOL FACTS ABOUT SKIN COLORS

- Polar bears have white fur, but their skin is black. Black skin is better for absorbing the heat from the sun, and it keeps polar bears warm in the arctic cold.

- The goldenrod spider will change the color of its skin from white to bright yellow to match the flower it rests on. This is a good way for the spider to stay hidden from the insects it's trying to catch for its next meal.

- Many other animals can quickly change the color of their skin. They include octopuses, flounders, sea horses, and chameleons. These animals use color changes for camouflage, which means they can match the color of a leaf or flower or twig to hide from predators or prey. In contrast, some animals change their skin color in ways that make them stand out so they can attract mates or signal danger.

Some Kids Tan and Some Kids Burn

Out in the sun, when it gets hot,
some kids get red and burn a lot.
Yet kids with darker skin shades can
stay in the sun and just get tan.

So, Dr. Jo, I'd like to learn
why some kids tan and some kids burn.
And kids who burn, what can they do
so that their skin will turn tan too?

We tan because of melanin—
you know, that stuff that colors skin.
It turns out melanin has ways
of blocking sunlight's UV rays.

If UV rays get in a cell,
they injure it and make it swell.
So, as a shield, skin will begin
to make some extra melanin.

UV rays from the sun

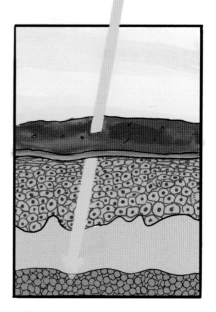

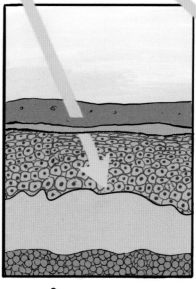

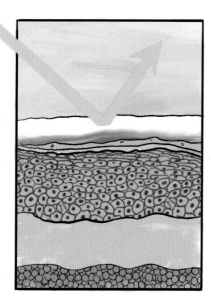

Pale, burned skin

Darker skin

Skin with sunscreen

This melanin builds up and can
spread through the skin so it looks tan.
A tanner skin will mean, in turn,
there's much less chance our skin will burn.

Now, kids with darker skin start out
with extra melanin throughout.
In sun, dark skin makes even *more*
and turns much darker than before.

But those kids with the lightest skin
can't produce enough melanin
to make their skin get tan; instead,
when they're in sun, they'll turn bright red.

Though tans protect, it has been found
we *all* need sunscreen smeared around.
'Cause even dark skin lets rays in,
and too much sun can damage skin.

COOL FACTS ABOUT SUNSCREENS

- Hippopotamuses make red sweat. Their skin produces a thick red fluid that protects them from UV sun rays. It also keeps away dangerous bacteria and some insects. Scientists are looking into ways of making a hippo gel that humans can use as sunscreen!

- Many tropical fishes, such as damselfish, produce a mucus that acts as sunscreen. This mucus protects them from burning when UV rays from the hot sun penetrate the water.

Freckles, Freckles Everywhere

I have these freckles everywhere.
My face, my arms. It's so unfair.
And when I'm outside in the sun,
I freckle more. It's never done.

So, Dr. Jo, just tell me, please,
what is the cause of all of these?
And should I worry? Should I care
if I have freckles everywhere?

All of those freckles can be seen
in folks that have a freckle gene.
Since Dad or Mom gave this to you,
then he or she might freckle too.

This gene is found most often in
the people with the palest skin.
And on those folks that have red hair,
you might see freckles everywhere!

The freckles come from melanin,
which, as you know, protects our skin
and builds up in our cells on days
when we're beneath the sun's strong rays.

This melanin spreads out and can
cause certain skin to look quite tan.
But in some folks, it doesn't spread,
but gathers into spots instead.

And frecklers have more freckly skin
in spots where lots of sun gets in.
So, extra freckles take their place
along the arms and on the face.

Your freckles are what make you *you*!
But one important thing to do
is put on sunscreen every day
before you go outside to play.

Sunscreen won't make you freckle-free,
but you'll have fewer spots, you'll see.
Those ones you got the other day
may naturally just fade away.

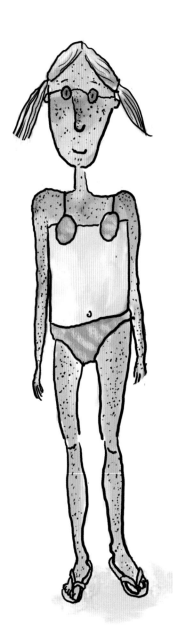

When I'm Embarrassed I Turn Red

Today my teacher called on me,
and it was plain for all to see
that both my cheeks had turned bright red.
I wished that I were home in bed.

Please, Dr. Jo, just tell me why
I can't stop blushing, though I try.
And why do I turn red and hot,
when other kids in class do not?

If you are nervous, then you might
release **adrenaline** to fight
your fear about just what to do
each time the teacher calls on you.

Adrenaline can help you flee
from any scary enemy
by getting extra blood to flow
into your legs to help you go.

As it turns out, another place
where extra blood goes is your face.
Though no one really knows quite why,
it's worse if you are kind of shy.

And, really, it's not only you
who blushes—but the red shows through
in light-skinned people, while in those
with darker skin, it hardly shows.

So take a deep breath when you blush
and slow way down, no need to rush.
Then think of something calm instead
and maybe you won't turn so red.

My Fingers Get White in the Snow

Sometimes when it's a snowy day,
if I take off my gloves to play,
my fingers get too cold and might
change color and look pale and white.

Please, Dr. Jo, why is it so?
Why do my fingers change in snow?
And if I warm them quickly, then
will they turn back to pink again?

The blood inside your hands will move
throughout each finger and each groove.
This brings fuel into every cell
and carries in some warmth as well.

When it got cold, your body tried
to hold all of your warmth inside.
If it had not, your heat would flow
out of each finger and each toe.

To keep you warm, blood vessels close
inside your fingers and your toes.
Less blood goes to your hands and feet.
And this way, you lose much less heat.

It's blood that makes your fingers pink.
So, when that blood flow starts to shrink,
your hands and all your fingers might
change color till they're pale or white.

So wear your gloves, for if you do,
you'll keep that heat inside of you.
They'll let the blood flow back, and then
your fingers will turn pink again.

COOL FACTS ABOUT KEEPING WARM

- Elephants stay warm when it gets cool by closing blood vessels in their ears. Their large ears provide a big surface that can let a lot of heat get out. When less of the warm blood goes into an elephant's ears, more can go to the rest of its body, keeping most of the animal nice and toasty.

- Ducks and other birds stand on ice by letting their feet get very, very cold. Meanwhile, they are able keep the rest of their bodies warm. They do this by using a special patch of blood vessels, which makes the heat in the blood that moves down their legs flow back up their legs and to their body before it ever gets to their feet.

PART III
SWEATY, BUMPY, WRINKLY SKIN

Your awesome skin can change a lot.
Sometimes it's wrinkly, sometimes not.
And fingerprints will always show,
while sweat and goose bumps come and go.

What makes skin change in all these ways?
And what about skin always stays?
The bumps and folds, what are they for?
Read on, and you will find out more!

My Fingerprints Give Me Away

"Enough with the cookies," my mother had said,
but I tiptoed downstairs before getting in bed.
Then I opened the jar, and I gobbled down two.
But by the next morning, my mother, she knew.

There wasn't too much I could actually say
because three little fingerprints gave me away.
So, please, Dr. Jo, tell me: Why do I find
that whenever I touch things, I leave prints behind?

Your hands and your fingers might look like they're clean,
but they're covered with stuff that's not easily seen.
Like the sweat that seeps out from the tiny **sweat glands**
that are found in the fingers on both of your hands.

But it isn't just sweat. Because each time you touch
anything with your hands, you just pick up so much:
like oils you get rubbing your face and your hair,
and the dust, grease, and dirt that are found everywhere.

This dirty sweat mixture is what Mom will find
when she sees all those prints that your hands left behind.
It sticks to the places you touched on the door,
and it also leaves marks on the wall and the floor.

So, if you wash up and you get your hands clean,
you'll still leave some prints, but they will not be seen.
You'd need to brush powders all over the door
to see all of those prints that you couldn't before.

Still, sneaking around with clean hands just won't do,
'cause when you snitch cookies, you'll still leave a clue:
The next time your mom goes to get you some more,
she'll notice the jar is less full than before!

COOL FACTS ABOUT FINGERPRINTS

- Each person has his or her own distinct set of fingerprints. These fingerprints form when a fetus is still growing in its mother's womb. Identical twins form similar fingerprints—but they are not *exactly* the same.

- Most animals do not have fingerprints, but chimpanzees, gorillas, and pandas all do. Panda fingerprints look very much like human fingerprints.

- Spider monkeys have tail prints! These ridges, which are found on the tips of their long tails, are important because spider monkeys use their tails as a third hand to grip and pick things up.

I've Got Blue Ink All Over Me

Sometimes when I write with a pen,
I twirl the pen around, and then
I hold my fingers up and see
I've got blue ink all over me!

I wash my hands, but it might stay
and stay and stay throughout the day.
So, Dr. Jo, could you please say
how I can make it go away?

Ink on your fingers starts to seep
into your cells, though not too deep.
Just through the upper layers in
the epidermis of your skin.

These upper cells of skin are dead.
And every day, thousands are shed,
as they are pushed off from below
by new skin cells that form and grow.

So, though it looks the same to you,
your upper skin is always new.
And quickly, sooner than you think,
you'll shed those cells that filled with ink.

My Fingers Wrinkle in the Pool

When I get hot and want to cool,
I play for hours in the pool.
Each time I do, small wrinkles show
on every finger and each toe.

But nothing else gets wrinkly,
at least as far as I can see.
My arms and legs are wrinkle-free.
My tummy's smooth as it can be.

Why, Dr. Jo, do wrinkles start,
but not on every single part?
And why is it they never stay?
What makes them quickly go away?

Your outer skin's protected by
a bit of oil, which keeps it dry.
Unless you're in the pool all day,
which makes the oil wash away.

Then water will seep through your skin,
which causes wrinkling to begin.
This **reflex** slows the blood that goes
into your fingers and your toes.

Since blood's what plumps your digits out,
they wrinkle up with less about.
These wrinkly fingers help your grip,
so things you touch won't slide and slip.

And also, scientists suppose,
all of those wrinkles on your toes
might help you when you walk around
along a wet and slippery ground.

But when you start to dry off, then
your skin oils will come back again,
and digits plump. Now they are much
more useful for your sense of touch.

'Cause when they're wrinkled, they do not
press down on every single spot.
So, probably, it's best we get
those wrinkles only when we're wet.

Goose Bumps Popped Up on My Skin

Last night I read a scary book
in bed, and that was all it took.
I soon felt chills, and I could see
that goose bumps had popped up on me.

They also show up sevenfold
when I am **shivering** in the cold.
All up my arms, most every place,
but never, ever on my face.

So, can you tell me, Dr. Jo,
what makes these goose bumps come and go?
And why only in certain places,
like our arms, but not our faces?

When you're cold or have a scare,
it actually affects your hair!
And you have hairs from head to toe,
though many of them hardly show.

If you are scared or even chilly,
muscles called **arrector pili**
tense around each little hair
and pull them up into the air.

Each hair then pulls a little bit
up on the skin surrounding it,
which makes those goose bumps form right there,
around the base of every hair.

But muscles near your facial hair
are really small; they're hardly there.
Since they don't really work at all,
your facial hair won't rise and fall.

When hairs don't rise, no goose bumps form,
and so this also is the norm
in places that have *no* hair strands—
like soles of feet and palms of hands.

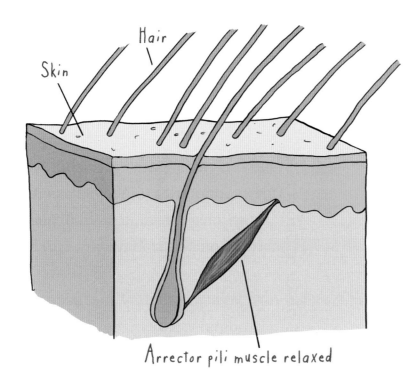

Skin

Hair

Arrector pili muscle relaxed

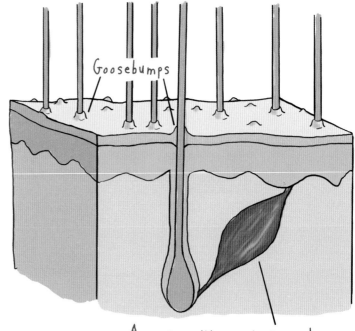

Goosebumps

Arrector pili muscle tensed

Now since our hairs can rise, you would
think that this movement does some good.
But as most human hair is thin,
it can't protect. It lets things in.

Not so for cats and dogs. When cold,
their thick hair raises up to hold
an extra pocket of trapped air,
which helps them keep some warmth in there.

Also, because cats are hairy,
when their hair's on end, it's scary!
So, when they feel threatened, they
can scare those scary things away.

But human hair is thin instead
(except in places like the head).
And tiny hairs won't hold our heat
or scare the people that we meet.

Our thin skin hairs, they don't do much,
except to help a bit with touch.
For if a breeze begins to blow,
our hairs will move, and we will know.

So, there you have it! Bumps appear
when you are cold or you feel fear.
They've got no purpose that we know.
They simply come, and then they go.

A COOL FACT ABOUT HAIRS THAT STAND ON END

• Porcupines use their arrector pili muscles to make their quills stand on end. That's pretty scary for anything that gets too close! And dangerous, too, because quills are modified hairs that can pull off and stick into the skin of a predator. It takes a porcupine several months to grow back a lost quill, but they have many thousands covering their skin, so the loss of a few is not a big deal.

Sweaty, Sweaty Me

When I get warm, then you can bet
I'll very quickly start to sweat.
It seems to come from every place:
my arms, my back, and down my face.

My forehead drips; my clothes get wet.
I simply cannot stand this sweat.
But my best friend—his name is Paul—
he hardly ever sweats at all.

So, Dr. Jo, please tell me why
I sweat so much, but Paul stays dry.
And why do I sweat everywhere?
I'm even sweaty in my hair!

You have two million sweat glands in
the **dermal regions** of your skin.
They're on your head, your arms, your toes,
and even on your chin and nose.

These glands, called sudoriferous,
make lots of sweat, and that's a plus.
Sweat cools you when you run and play
or stay out in the sun all day.

When you are in a sweaty state,
your sweat will soon **evaporate**.
Which means some of the sweat that's there
moves off your skin into the air.

And every sweat drop holds within
a little heat from off your skin.
So, when sweat leaves, the heat goes too—
and then that heat comes off of *you*.

One reason that you get so wet,
while Paul just doesn't seem to sweat,
might simply be that he was born
someplace that wasn't very warm.

If you grew up where it is hot,
then you will likely have a lot
of active sweat glands, while your friend
has fewer working in the end.

Another cause for sweat can be
strong feelings of anxiety.
When you are nervous, you can get
a racing heart and lots of sweat.

It's how your body deals with fear:
it revs things up when danger's near.
So if you run, and get real hot,
that sweat will cool you down a lot.

COOL FACTS ABOUT SWEAT GLANDS

- Your lips are one of the few places on your skin that have no sweat glands.

- There are more than two million sweat glands in your skin. The palms of your hands have the most, with more than three thousand sweat glands per square inch. (A square inch is a little bigger than the size of a quarter.) Your feet have lots of sweat glands too, and these glands work to make your hands and feet a little wet to help you get a better grip, or to help you run barefoot.

- Pigs have very few working sweat glands, so they cannot use sweat to get cool. Instead, they wallow in mud on hot days.

- Cats and dogs have sweat glands only on their paws and in their noses. They can't make a lot of sweat from these, so they cool down by panting instead of sweating.

- Animals that run, like dogs, cats, rats, and mice, have sweat glands in their foot pads. This helps them run without slipping. Rabbits, who hop, have none.

We're Getting Stinky

Out in the school yard yesterday,
I smelled my friends and walked away.
The stink I smelled was just so strong
I simply had to move along.

Then someone else I knew quite well
said, "Did you know you really smell?"
And there it was. I finally knew
that my friends think *I'm* stinky too.

Please, Dr. Jo, just tell me why
most every girl and every guy—
and that includes myself, I think—
has suddenly begun to stink?

And I can't smell myself at all,
at least as far as I recall.
So tell me too, how it can be,
I smell my friends, but they smell me?

One of the things that you will see
as kids start reaching **puberty**
is very soon they will begin
to have a stinky, sweaty skin.

At puberty, some sweat glands get
to make a special kind of sweat.
These special smelly sweat glands hide
within your armpits, deep inside.

(Your other sweat glands aren't at fault;
they just make water with some salt.
This sweat won't smell much, as a rule.
It's only there to keep you cool.)

Now, armpit sweat, it has been shown,
does not have much smell on its own.
But it's got fats and proteins, too,
that mix to form a stinky brew.

Bacteria from your own skin
will join, and quickly mix right in
and break sweat down so that you get
that extra-smelly armpit sweat.

But **smell receptors** react more
to smells they've never smelled before,
and if a smell just stays around,
your smell receptors dial it down.

Now, since your own smell's always there,
your smellers won't make you aware.
But other folks may notice it
if you should have a smelly pit.

So, if you want to lose that scent,
start using some deodorant!

COOL FACTS ABOUT SMELLY SWEAT

- A day after you eat garlic, other folks may smell it in your sweat and on your breath. That's because chemicals in garlic include **sulfur compounds** that are broken down in the digestive tract to form a smelly chemical called allyl methyl sulfide (AMS). AMS gets into the blood, where it's carried to the lungs and sweat. It takes many hours to digest garlic and for the AMS to form and travel, so the stink won't be detected right away. And you won't smell it on yourself at all. That's because the smell receptors in your nose turn off quickly to odors that stick around. Our receptors respond most strongly to new smells or smells that change.

- Mosquitoes can locate humans by sensing smelly compounds in their sweat. Some of the chemicals that mosquitoes particularly like include **ammonia** and **lactic acid**.

- Skunks have **apocrine sweat glands** around their **anuses** that put out a strong stinky musk scent. Skunks also have muscles attached to these glands that allow them to squirt the musk out into the air, right onto an intruder. Watch out!

PART IV
CUT, BRUISED, SCABBY SKIN

Each time you scrape or cut your skin,
a healing process will begin.
Your skin may scab or form a bruise,
but underneath, the skin renews.

In this next section, I'll show you
amazing things your skin can do
to make a cut or scrape or tear
soon look like it was never there!

I Cut My Thumb

I cut my thumb, and ouch, it hurts!
The blood comes out in drops, not spurts.
A bandage made it stop, but then
I took it off and bled again.

Please, Dr. Jo, I need to know
why, once the blood begins to flow,
a bandage stops it very fast,
but if I move, it doesn't last.

And please, what can I do that would
make all the bleeding stop for good?
This silly bandage looks so dumb!
When can I take it off my thumb?

When your cut bleeds, it means that you
have cut a capillary through.
But your blood has the things you need
to close the hole and stop the bleed.

A speedy process will begin:
the **platelets** that the blood brings in
stick to the capillary's hole
and form a plug to get control.

This **platelet plug** is not that strong.
It holds in blood but won't last long,
and wiggling your thumb about
can make that little plug pop out.

The platelet plug is the first part.
But pretty soon, your blood will start
to build a stronger, tougher **clot**
that forms around the injured spot.

The clot has **fibrin threads** that wind
between the platelets so they bind
to tightly fill the open space
and form a patch that stays in place.

It takes at least five minutes, though,
for fibrin threads to form and grow.
Eventually, you'll have enough
to make a clot that's strong and tough.

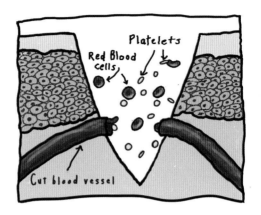

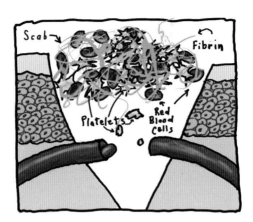

So leave the bandage, if you're smart,
to let the **clotting process** start.
'Cause if you hit your thumb, it may
push at the clot so it won't stay.

It may take a few weeks, but then
you'll have completely normal skin.
No matter how you search that spot,
you'll never know there was a clot.

A COOL FACT ABOUT BLOOD CLOTTING

- Bloodsucking animals like mosquitoes, ticks, leeches, and bats all have chemicals in their saliva that keep blood from clotting for a little while. These chemicals prevent clotting only in the small area where the bloodsucker has cut into a blood vessel. The anticlotting chemicals hang around just long enough to allow the animal to suck up a tasty blood meal before the victim's blood washes them all away.

Black and Blue and Yellow, Too

Last week a baseball hit *my* arm,
and now I see, with some alarm,
the spot it hit turned black and blue,
and purple, brown, and yellow, too.

It doesn't hurt, but it's so strange
how every day, the colors change.
Mom says it's healing—it's okay—
but will it ever go away?

Please, Dr. Jo, can you explain
this nasty bruise, when there's no pain?
And why's it purple, blue, and brown.
What's going on way deep, deep down?

A smack against your skin can make
small capillaries tear and break.
And if you don't cut *through* the skin,
the blood you bleed just stays within.

Around your skin cells, leaked blood flows
and makes that large red bruise that shows.
The red's from hemoglobin that
turns red when oxygen's attached.

But oxygen's not there for long.
Skin cells absorb it; soon it's gone.
This changes hemoglobin's hue,
which now, through skin, looks purply blue.

Up next: the hemoglobin breaks
down into smaller parts and makes
those other colors that you've found:
we'll look at green, yellow, and brown.

The hemoglobin slowly changes
as its structure rearranges,
till it forms the next thing seen,
called **biliverdin**, which is green.

Bilirubin next is made;
it gives your skin that yellow shade.
And last is **hemosiderin**,
which will look brown inside your skin.

While all those colors are what show,
skin cells beneath them quickly grow.
As bruises heal, there's no more pain—
but colored stuff can still remain.

Just give it time, and you will find
there's no more leaked blood left behind.
This means that in a week or two,
you won't see red or brown or blue.

Stages of how a bruise heals

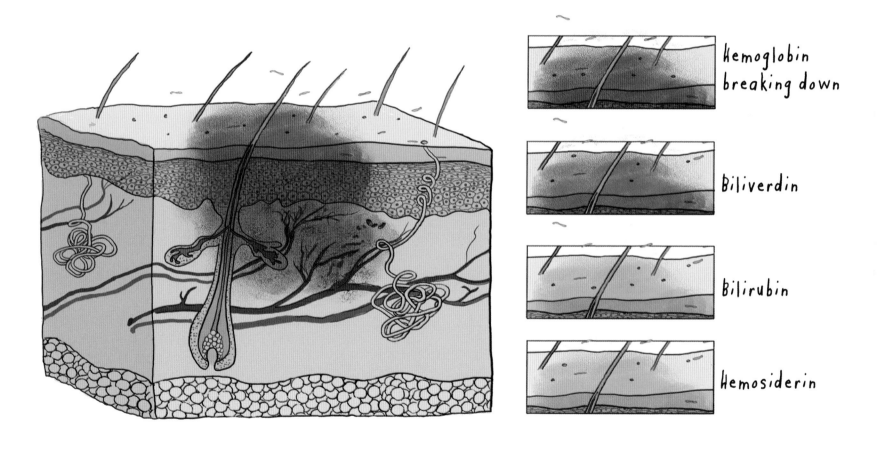

Hemoglobin breaking down

Biliverdin

Bilirubin

Hemosiderin

COOL FACTS ABOUT HEMOGLOBIN

- Yellow urine and brown feces get their colors from hemoglobin too. Our old **red blood cells**, which have hemoglobin inside them, die and get replaced by new ones. The dying red cells are broken down, and just like with a bruise, red hemoglobin changes into different compounds that go on to make urine yellow, or feces brown.

- Unlike humans, who always bleed red blood, some animals bleed blue blood. These include crabs, shrimp, octopuses, scorpions, and some spiders. Their blood contains blue hemocyanin instead of red hemoglobin. Hemocyanin is like hemoglobin, because it also carries oxygen to cells.

- A few animals bleed bright green blood! These include lizards from New Guinea called green tree skinks, a few kinds of fish called sculpins, and certain green frogs from Cambodia. Their green blood comes from biliverdin. As you know, biliverdin is formed in our own blood when hemoglobin breaks down, and it makes our bruises look green.

I've Got a Scab I Want to Pick

I hate this scab; it's ugly, ick!
It really makes me want to pick.
But Mom says leave the scab alone,
it's going to drop off on its own.

Please tell me why it's not okay
to simply peel this scab away.
I really do not think it's fair.
I want to see what's under there.

A scab is really just the top
of an old blood clot, there to stop
the bleeding from a cut or nick.
It helps you heal. Please do not pick!

Scabs quickly dry, so soon enough
it's going to feel quite hard and rough.
And red cells from the blood you bled
will make the scab look dark and red.

A scab gives time for healing skin
to grow and fill the spaces in,
so that in just a week or two,
the skin below the scab is new.

This growing skin keeps moving up
and pushing at the scab on top,
so that it loosens every day
until it simply drops away.

So here's a message you should heed:
Don't pick your scab, 'cause it might bleed.
And then it will just form once more,
replacing what you had before.

PART V
ITCHY, SIZZLING, PEELING SKIN

How do mosquitoes decide which
of us bite, and make us itch?
And how does sun from yesterday
still make our skin feel hot today?

Why do we peel and want to pick,
or shiver when we're hot and sick?
In this next section, we'll explore
the itch, the peel, and so much more!

Mosquitoes Love Me!

Mosquitoes bite me so much more
than they bite *my* friend Eleanor.
I get bites on *my* hands and nose
and even on *my* shoeless toes.

Why do mosquitoes love *me* so?
I really, really want to know.
It might sound mean, but in the end
I'd rather they would love *my* friend!

Mosquitoes are attracted to
a gas that's known as **CO_2**.
You breathe it out, and they fly in
when they detect it near your skin.

Then very soon, they're close enough
that their antennae sense more stuff.
Ammonia, lactic acid, too—
all in the sweat that comes from you.

Our sweat all looks the same, and yet
we each make slightly different sweat.
And though you may not smell *your* smell,
mosquitoes sense it very well.

Where a mosquito lands depends
on who among your nearby friends
gives off the sweat that carries more
of what these pests are looking for.

So there *is* something you can do
when those mosquitoes buzz near you:
Just stay close to a friend you're sure
the blood suckers will like much more!

COOL FACTS ABOUT MOSQUITOES

- Only female mosquitoes feed on blood from other animals. Blood contains nutrients that the females need so their eggs can grow and mature. But it's hard to get a lot of energy-rich sugar out of blood, so adult female mosquitoes don't use blood for energy. Instead, like male mosquitoes, they suck up sweet plant nectars for sugar.

- Mosquitoes that live in cold places like Alaska will hibernate, or go into a slowed-down, sleeplike state, for as long as eight months. They become active and bloodsucking again when it gets warm.

- Active (nonhibernating) adult mosquitoes have very short lives. Male mosquitoes only live for about one week. Females of different species (there are more than three thousand mosquito species in the world) live from anywhere between two weeks and three months, not including hibernating time.

- Mosquitoes pick up your scent from as far as one hundred feet away. That's equal to a little more than the length of a basketball court, or the length of two and a half school buses.

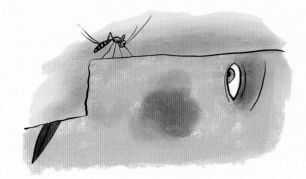

I'm So Itchy

What's with this huge mosquito bite?
It's on my face. It's quite a sight.
An itchy, bumpy, big red patch
that mother says I should not scratch.

It makes me crazy, Dr. J!
I want to scratch and scratch all day.
Why does this bug bite itch so much?
And why is it so wrong to touch?

When that mosquito comes and feeds
upon your blood, the thing it needs
is for the blood to flow and flow
and not form clots that make blood slow.

It pokes its sharp **proboscis** in
through many layers of your skin,
and shoots saliva through your very
tiny, blood-filled capillary.

That saliva's going to come
with chemicals that make you numb,
and others that work in that spot
to make sure blood won't form a clot.

Next, the insect drinks a lot,
while you can't feel it there to swat.
But meantime, working sight unseen,
your cells are making **histamine**.

This histamine makes vessels leak
blood's **plasma**, which will start to sneak
into the spaces round your cells
so skin turns red and hard and swells.

The plasma's there so that it may
wash all that insect juice away.
And next, **white blood cells** will break down
mosquito juice that's left around.

The most annoying thing is this:
that histamine will make you itch.
And if you scratch to calm things down,
more histamine will spread around.

Though histamine's a pain today,
it will break down and seep away.
So though it's quite hard to resist,
you really shouldn't scratch that itch.

Ouch! I've Got a Sunburn

I spent all Tuesday at the pool.
The games were great, the water cool.
I went inside to get a drink,
and I could see my skin was pink.

I wasn't worried, not a bit.
I hardly even noticed it.
But then that night, from toes to head,
my skin had turned from pink to red.

And right around the reddest spot,
my skin was very, very hot.
What's worse, my socks, my pants, my shirt
rubbed on that skin and made it hurt.

Please, Dr. Jo, I need to learn
why does my skin get red and burn,
and why is it the worst burns come
long after I've been in the sun?

The sun gives out its energy
in part as light, which we can see,
and partly as unnoticed rays
that touch our skin in different ways.

Like **infrareds**, which make us hot.
Though it turns out these rays are not
what make skin burn and turn bright red:
It's **ultraviolet rays**, instead.

When ultraviolet rays get in,
they penetrate cells in your skin.
Then chemicals from each pierced cell
make tiny capillaries swell,

and extra blood leaks out to form
an **inflamed** spot that's red and warm.
The leaked blood helps your skin to deal
with injured cells so it can heal.

It brings in white blood cells to do
the job of your skin's cleanup crew.
They gobble up each injured cell
and clear out any germs as well.

Then white cells in the injured spot
attract *more* white cells, quite a lot,
while **kinins** from your damaged cells
draw more leaked blood in so skin swells.

These white cells and leaked blood remain
and press on nerve cells, causing pain.
And all those kinins also make
your pain cells fire, so burns ache.

This all takes time. So you won't see
your burn when you are out at three.
But your skin might be sore and red
at night, when you climb into bed.

Then after just a day or two,
there's not much cleanup left to do,
so white cells and leaked blood can then
move back into your veins again.

Soon skin's not swollen, red, or sore
and looks just like it did before.
But frequent burns cause damage in
the very deepest parts of skin.

So, next time you are in the sun,
be sure to play and have some fun,
but smear on sunscreen every place:
your arms, your legs, and on your face.

A cap, some shade, and long sleeves, too
can keep that hot sun off of you.
And keep in mind the sunscreen rule:
apply more when you leave the pool.

COOL FACTS ABOUT SUNBURNS

- Animals can get sunburned just like people do. Those that live in very sunny places will have protective fur, feathers, or scales; but animals like dogs or cats that have short hair and light-colored skin can get burns. And sea animals, like beached whales that get stuck out of the water, can get burned from too much sun.

- You can get a sunburn on a cloudy day. Though clouds that cover the sun may keep out some ultraviolet radiation, rays can still get through. So, you still need sunscreen when you play outside in cloudy weather, even when you don't feel the hot sun beating down on you.

I'm Losing My Skin!

A sunburn I got Saturday
has lost its red and gone away.
But now on Monday, though I feel
less sore, my skin's begun to peel.

Please, Dr. Jo, can you explain
why skin comes off, yet there's no pain?
And when skin peels, what happens then?
Will all of it grow back again?

It's normal that each day we shed
our upper skin cells, which are dead.
These epidermal skin cells die
while deeper skin cells multiply.

Dead cells are small, so you can't see
them form in clumps of two or three,
which, by the thousands, every day,
come off your skin and float away.

But when you burn, sun rays attack
those *deeper* cells inside the stack.
These deeper cells die in a glop,
which quickly moves up to the top.

In time, these gloppy cells break free
in flaky sheets that you can see.
And while that skin begins to peel,
the skin below will start to heal.

So peeling skin is no disaster.
In response, cells just grow faster
than they normally would do,
making your skin look good as new.

COOL FACTS ABOUT PEELING SKIN

- Snakes shed their entire outer layer of skin all at once. Their skin layer peels from nose to tail, and includes the covering over their eyes. It takes at least seven days for a snake to shed its skin; meanwhile, the snake's new skin forms underneath. Young snakes will do this one or two times a month. Older snakes shed only once or twice a year.

- When a predator grabs an African spiny mouse, it can end up with a mouthful of skin, but no mouse. The spiny mouse can easily shed more than half of the skin on its back when grabbed. Then, while the predator chews on skin, the mouse scampers away. The spiny critter quickly replaces its lost skin and is completely back to normal in three days!

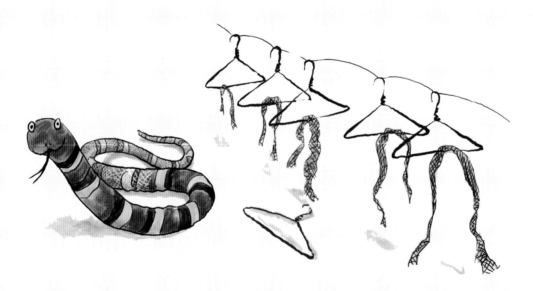

My Skin Is Hot, But I Feel Cold

My skin feels hot, or so I'm told.
But I feel very, very cold.
My temperature's a hundred two,
but I think I am turning blue!

I pile the covers extra tall,
but that *just* doesn't help at all.
My arms are shivering hard, and yet,
my forehead is all drenched in sweat.

It really isn't very nice
to feel like you're a block of ice.
Please, Dr. Jo, it's getting old.
How can I be both hot and cold?

When you get sick, your body tries
to kill the nasty germs that hide
inside your skin, your gut, your nose,
and anywhere that your blood flows.

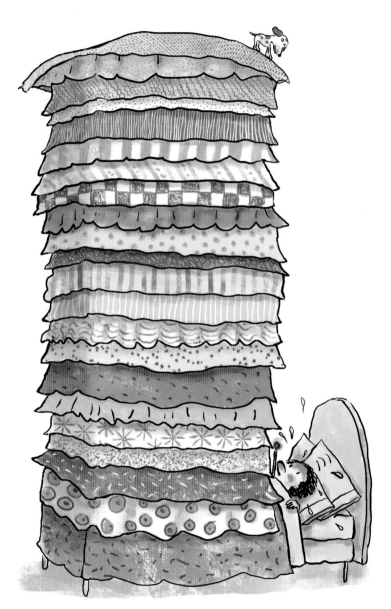

And so your brain says, "Make it hot!"
because those mean old germs cannot
survive and thrive and multiply
when temperatures are very high.

A special region of your brain,
the **hypothalamus**, is to blame
for resetting your body's core
to ninety-nine degrees or more.

And so, here is the funny thing:
your brain will start you shivering
to try and get you warm enough
to raise your temperature way up.

And now your body "feels" cold, too.
This way, the brain makes sure that you
eat soup and pile the blankets high,
cause when you're hot, the germs will die.

Then, once those germs cannot attack,
your hypothalamus sets things back
to **normal temperatures**. And then
you'll sweat to cool back down again.

COOL FACTS ABOUT BODY TEMPERATURES

- Arctic ground squirrels, which live in very cold places like Alaska and Siberia, have body temperatures that drop down to 26°F. That is colder than ice. They let their bodies cool down when they go into hibernation in the winter. This makes these squirrels the coldest living mammals on earth. In the spring, when they wake up, the ground squirrels quickly raise their body temperatures back up to their normal 97.5°F.

- Round-tailed ground squirrels, which live in the desert, can let their body temperatures get up to 107°F and still run around normally.

PART VI
PIMPLY, BLISTERED, WARTY SKIN

One morning you might find that you
have pimples, maybe quite a few.
Or nasty bumps of other sorts,
like blisters or those ugly warts.

Why does your skin so suddenly
form big red bumps for all to see?
What caused that blister, wart, or pimple?
I'll explain and keep it simple.

I've Got a Pimple on My Nose

I've got a pimple on my nose.
It seems like every day it grows.
And worst of all, it's found a place
right in the middle of my face.

So, Dr. Jo, I need to know!
What makes an ugly pimple grow?
And can you tell me, when you're through,
why I have **white-** and **blackheads,** too?

A little pimple can begin
to form on extra-oily skin.
Your skin makes oils every day—
but too much oil gets in the way.

Your **oil glands** are everywhere,
right at the root of each small hair.
These glands work hard to grease the skin,
to keep it smooth and moist within.

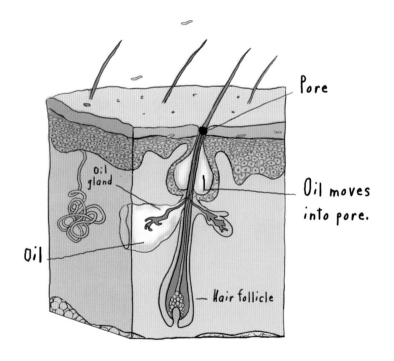

Pore

Oil moves into pore.

oil gland

Oil

— Hair follicle

WHITEHEAD

Oil-filled pore

Oil gland

hair follicle

BLACKHEAD

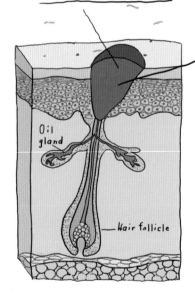

Oil, dirt, and dead skin cells fill pore.

Oil gland

hair follicle

Your hairs grow through a **pore** so small,
you'd hardly know it's there at all.
There's also oil inside that pore—
a tiny bit, and not much more.

But sometimes glands make oil at such
a fast pace that there's way too much.
Then pores can clog beneath the skin,
and whitehead pimples form within.

Now, blackheads form when there is *more*
than extra oil stuck in a pore.
'Cause sometimes oil can form a goo,
and germs can get stuck in there too.

Plus dead skin cells will mix inside,
and push the pore to open wide.
The goop is now exposed to air,
which breaks down cells and oils in there.

Those dead cells contain melanin,
which mixes with the oils and then
creates that tiny, dark brown spot.
(You'll think it's dirt, but it is not.)

Now when kids start to reach their teens,
they make more **hormones**—and this means
their oil glands get revved up too,
and soon those pimply bumps show through.

Your oil glands work hardest in
your nose, your forehead, and your chin.
And washing may not be enough
to keep off all the oily stuff.

But as your hormones settle down,
far fewer pimples come around.
And know it isn't only you;
most other kids have pimples too!

A COOL FACT ABOUT PIMPLES

- Animals can get pimples too. Cats can get them on their chins. Dogs with short hair, like boxers and bulldogs, can get pimples all over. Normally, this happens when they reach puberty—just like with people. Dogs reach puberty at five to eight months of age. Dog pimples usually disappear at one year of age, when the dog is fully mature.

I've Got a Blister on My Toe

I got some new shoes, Dr. Jo;
they caused a blister on my toe.
And now I really must complain.
Each time I walk, my toe's in pain.

So, Dr. Jo, I'd like to know
what made this ugly blister grow.
I'd love to pop this thing today.
Will popping make it go away?

A blister often forms within
those places where you have thick skin,
like on your fingers or your toes
(but rarely on your arms and nose).

It happens when skin in one spot
gets rubbed and rubbed and rubbed a lot
so that the skin cells in that place
will separate, and leave a space.

Then fluid from surrounding skin
flows all around and seeps right in.
And that's what makes the blister grow
into that bubble on your toe.

A thick skin cover will protect
the blister from what might infect
the irritated cells below—
a place you don't want germs to go.

So, if you should decide to pop
your blister, and you rip the top,
you'll need some **antiseptic** there.
And then please bandage it with care.

It's possible to pop it so
the cover stays and germs can't grow.
But better yet, leave it alone,
'cause it will heal up on its own.

Below the blister, skin cells hide,
and they are working to divide
and make new skin cells to replace
the ones that once filled up that space.

Meanwhile, be careful, and make sure
your shoes don't rub there anymore.
A bandage is what you should use.
And next time, try some different shoes!

A COOL FACT ABOUT BLISTERS

- Blister beetles can give other animals blisters. These beetles make a chemical called cantharidin that causes blisters to form in animals that eat them. Sometimes cows and horses accidentally swallow these nasty beetles when they feed on crops like alfalfa, which the beetles are fond of, and then they can get blisters both inside and out. Gross!

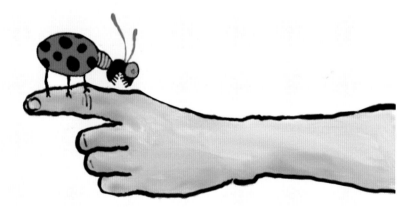

I Hate This Wart

I've got this wart, it's quite a pip.
It sticks up on my fingertip.
It's very lumpy, rough, and wide,
and seems to have black seeds inside.

Oh, Dr. Jo, I'd like to know
what makes these nasty wart bumps grow.
And why is it that I'm the sort
to get this stupid, ugly wart?

A **virus** known as **HPV**
is what has caused that wart you see.
This virus can get buried in
a cut or nick that's in your skin.

Wart viruses are everywhere:
the shower, floor, a desk or chair,
a person's hand, a door, a tree.
They all might carry HPV.

Inside the epidermal parts
of skin is where the virus starts.
It gets in cells that don't divide,
and changes them, way deep inside.

These changed cells now divide in clumps
and form those little warty bumps
which often fill with small black dots
that look like little dirty spots.

But they're not dirt, they're just what show
when extra capillaries grow
to feed the wart, and then shrink back
and leave behind a bit of black.

A wart's **contagious**, so do not
let it get near an injured spot,
such as a cut that's on your hand,
'cause that is where new warts may land.

And though warts can be spread by touch,
some folks don't seem to get warts much.
They might have an **immunity**
that helps them keep their skin wart-free.

If warts annoy you, your doc may
use stuff that freezes warts away
or chemicals she can apply
to make those ugly wart cells die.

But warts are harmless, have no fear!
And in some months—sometimes a year—
your warts should vanish on their own
if you can just leave them alone.

A COOL FACT ABOUT WARTS

- People cannot get warts from rubbing the bumps on the skin of toads. These large bumps are also called warts, but they are not the same as warts that people get. Toad warts are really small glands that make poisonous chemicals, which irritate any animal that touches or swallows them. These chemicals are nasty enough to keep predators at a safe distance.

CONCLUSION
YOUR SKIN WILL THANK YOU, THAT'S FOR SURE!

There are some days when you'll complain,
"This skin of mine is such a pain!
It itches, burns, and makes me sweat.
It peels and makes those zits I get."

But what's amazing is your skin
keeps making new cells from within.
Those bites and pimples go away.
And skin protects you every day!

So here are things that you can do
to help your skin take care of you.
Don't pick that scab, or scratch that bite,
or wear shoes that are way too tight.

You can rub lotion all about
to keep your skin from drying out.
And when you're outside having fun,
remember, sunscreen blocks that sun.

If you take care, your skin gives back,
and it won't blister, dry, or crack,
or burn and get all red and sore.
Your skin will thank you, that's for sure!

GLOSSARY

Adrenaline: Adrenaline is one of many chemicals, called "hormones," that are made by our bodies and released into our blood. Adrenaline is made when we are scared or excited. One thing it does is to bring in more blood to the muscles and get them to make extra energy so that, if we need to, we can fight or run away from danger very quickly.

Ammonia: Ammonia is a gas with a very strong smell. One type of ammonia is used in cleaning and is what gives some floor cleaners their scent. We give off a small amount of ammonia in our sweat.

Antiseptic: Antiseptics are chemicals that we put on a cut or wound to keep bacteria, viruses, and other invading organisms from getting in and causing an infection.

Anuses: The anus is the opening at the end of the large intestine. Feces with waste materials from digestion come out through the anus.

Apocrine sweat glands: Apocrine sweat glands are found in the genital areas and armpits. They produce a fatty sweat that combines with bacteria in the air and becomes smelly. The sweat glands found on the rest of the body are called eccrine sweat glands. Eccrine sweat glands make a thin sweat that is usually scentless.

Arrector pili: The arrector pili is a small muscle that is attached to each of the millions of hairs that cover our bodies. These muscles are involuntary. This means we can't just decide to make them contract. When we are cold or scared, our nervous system makes the arrector pili muscles contract automatically, causing our hairs to stand on end.

Biliverdin, bilirubin, hemosiderin: All these different compounds can be formed when hemoglobin gets broken down in the body. They are different colors, and they add color to bruises.

Blackheads: A blackhead forms when a hair follicle gets clogged with extra oil and dead skin cells. The clog widens the opening to the follicle so that the oily mass is open to oxygen in the air. This causes the melanin in the dead skin cells and oils in the pimple to break down and make the clogged follicle look black.

Capillary(ies): Capillaries are very tiny blood vessels that run everywhere in the body. They are so tiny that you can only see them with a microscope. They have very thin walls so that things like oxygen and sugars can move out of them to hungry cells in the tissues of your body. Wastes from these tissue cells also move *into* the capillaries and get carried away by your blood.

Carotene: Carotene is one kind of pigment that adds a yellow or orange shade to the browns and pinks of our skin. It also gives color to foods like carrots and sweet potatoes.

Cells divide: Skin cells divide or split into two cells when they are growing. This splitting of old cells to form new ones is called cell division. In the epidermis, only the very bottom layer of cells divides. This growth makes new cells that push up the cells above. All the upper cells are dying or dead.

Clot: A clot is a plug that forms to heal a cut blood vessel. It is made from things in the blood like fibrin threads, red blood cells, and platelets.

Clotting process: The clotting process is the way our blood keeps from leaking out of a cut blood vessel. In takes place in several steps. In the last step, blood forms a clot, which plugs up the cut.

CO_2: CO_2 is a gas that our cells give off when they break down sugar for energy. CO_2 is picked up by the blood and carried to the lungs, where it moves out with our breath. Mosquitoes are attracted to the CO_2 we breathe.

Collagen: Collagen fibers are thin threads of protein. Collagen is found in tissues all over the body, in places such as our skin, bones, blood vessels, and stomach. It is strong and stretchy and allows tissues to stretch and spring back again.

Contagious: A contagious virus or bacteria can be spread from one person to another. The virus that causes warts can pass easily between people by touch, so we say it is contagious. Cold viruses are contagious because they can be spread to another person when you sneeze.

Dermal regions or **dermis:** The dermis is the lower part of our skin. It is the place where sweat glands, oil glands, hair follicles, and blood vessels are found. Blood vessels bring in nutrients like oxygen and sugars. These nutrients seep out of the blood vessels and up into the cells of the epidermis.

Diffuse: Things diffuse when they move from a starting spot where there is a lot of them, and spread out to places where there isn't. This happens with things like oxygen, carbon dioxide, sugars, and fats. It happens in the air, in a liquid, or in a solid. In skin, oxygen, sugars, and other nutrients diffuse out from the blood vessels up to the skin cells. You can see diffusion in action by putting a drop of food coloring in a glass of water and watching the food coloring diffuse, or spread, through the water until it is mixed through the whole glass.

Epidermis: The epidermis is the very top part of the skin. It is made up of at least forty layers of skin cells, stacked like pancakes, one on top of the other. The very bottom layer has new growing cells. Most of the other layers have cells that are dead or dying. Skin that peels off after a sunburn is made up of dead cells from the epidermis.

Evaporate: Evaporation is the movement of some of a liquid's molecules—the building blocks that make up everything—out of the liquid. When water evaporates from the skin, water molecules move off the skin into the air.

Fibrin threads: Fibrins are sticky threads of protein that hold a blood clot together.

Follicles: A follicle is a package of cells that surrounds the part of a hair that is inside the skin. A hair grows up from the base, or bottom, of the follicle.

Genes: Genes are molecules inside our cells that direct everything our cells do. Through this direction, our genes affect everything about who we are, how we look, how our brains work, and how our bodies grow and develop.

Hemoglobin: Hemoglobin is a chemical in our red blood cells that carries oxygen from our lungs to the tissue cells in all the organs in our bodies. When hemoglobin picks up oxygen, it changes from a bluish-red to a bright red color. When we bleed, the hemoglobin picks up oxygen in the air and turns our blood bright red.

Histamine: Histamine is a chemical that helps the body fight bacteria and other invading organisms. It is made by certain kinds of white blood cells in our blood and tissues.

Hormones: Hormones are chemicals made in our bodies and released into our blood to control different things. Some hormones control our heart rate, others control hunger and digestion, and still others control the growth of our bones and muscles. In teenagers, the sex hormones estrogen and testosterone increase and make our oil glands release more oils. This can cause pimples to form. Sex hormones also cause the physical changes that occur in adolescence, like the growth of beards and extra muscle tissue in boys, and the development of breasts and widening of hips in girls.

HPV: HPV, or the *human papillomavirus*, is a virus that can infect our skin cells. This virus can cause warts by making skin cells grow extra quickly, forming a rough, bumpy patch of skin.

Hypodermis: The hypodermis is a layer of tissue located just below the dermis of skin. By binding to the dermis, the hypodermis helps to hold the skin in place. The hypodermis is filled with fat cells that help to keep us warm. Although this fatty layer is attached to the skin, it is not actually considered part of the skin. The hypodermis can also be called the "subcutaneous layer."

Hypothalamus: The hypothalamus is a part of the brain that is in charge of many bodily functions, including heart rate, hunger, and thirst. The hypothalamus also keeps track of changes in body temperature and makes us shiver if we get too cold and sweat if we get too warm.

Immunity: Immunity is the ability of our bodies to fight off an invading virus or bacteria before it makes us sick. If you get sick once with a specific kind of virus, like a chicken pox virus, your body starts making chemicals that can prevent that one type of virus from coming back again.

Inflamed/inflammation: An inflammation is the way the body deals with nearly any kind of injury. A cut, an invading microorganism, or an irritation can cause an inflammation. The inflamed region gets red, swollen, and warm when extra blood moves into the injured place. This extra blood brings in fluid and white blood cells to help heal a wound and fight off any invaders.

Infrared(s): Infrared radiation is one form of invisible energy from sunlight that reaches the Earth. Though we can't see it, we can feel it as heat, and its energy can be useful to make things work. For example, the remote control for your television uses infrared waves to turn it on and off and change the channels.

Kinins: Kinins are chemicals released by cut or burned cells in the body. Kinins help bring white blood cells to the injured spot so the process of healing can begin. They also stimulate pain cells to fire. The pain they cause is important because it lets you know to be careful not to hit, rub, or step on the injury.

Lactic acid: Lactic acid is a chemical that's left behind when active muscle cells need to break down sugar very quickly for a burst of energy. The lactic acid still has some leftover energy packed inside it. Muscles store some of this leftover energy and use it later, while they are resting, breaking down the lactic acid very slowly. But some lactic acid is never used, and is instead released as waste in our sweat.

Melanin: Melanin is a pigment; a chemical that has color. Melanins come in several forms. They may be yellow-red or blackish-brown. They are found in our skin cells and give color to our skin.

Melanocytes: Melanocytes are cells in the epidermis of our skin that make melanin. The melanin they make is sent out in packets and picked up by other skin cells.

Normal temperatures: The normal temperature for the human body is around 98.7°F. People start to get dangerously cold when their body temperature drops below 95°F, and they are in real trouble below 82°F. Humans are also in trouble if their temperature rises above 104°F. But other mammals differ greatly in how warm or cold their bodies can get.

Nutrient(s): Nutrients come from the food we eat, and we need them to be healthy. They include sugars, fats, proteins, vitamins, and minerals. After food is broken down in the stomach and intestines, the nutrients from the food are picked up by our blood and carried to our cells. Our cells use the nutrients for energy to keep our bodies running.

Oil glands: Oil glands (also called "sebaceous glands") are packets of cells in skin that make oils. Every hair on your body has its own oil gland. The oils from these glands help to keep your skin and hair from drying out.

Organ: An organ is a structure in the body with two or more kinds of tissues that work together to do a particular job. Your stomach, for example, is an organ made up of layers of tissues that enable the stomach to digest your food. Other organs include your heart, liver, skin, brain, and even your blood vessels.

Oxygen: Oxygen is a gas that is found in the air we breathe. It is picked up in our lungs by the hemoglobin in our blood. It is then carried to our bodies' cells, which use it to make energy.

Pigment: A pigment is a chemical that gives color to a cell or tissue. Pigments in our skin include melanins and carotenes.

Plasma: Plasma is the liquid part of the blood.

Platelet plug: A platelet plug is a clump of platelets that stick to a cut in a blood vessel. This plug keeps blood from leaking out while a stronger clot has time to form.

Platelets: Platelets are little bits of blood cells that float in the blood. When a blood vessel is cut, platelets stick to the cut and form a plug, and then these platelets release chemicals to form a more solid clot.

Pore(s): Pores are openings in the skin. Each hair comes out of the skin through its own pore. The pore is actually the opening to a package of cells, called a follicle, which protects the hair deep inside the skin.

Proboscis: The proboscis of a mosquito is a long, tube-shaped mouthpart. It includes sharp cutting blades that can pierce its victim's skin. It also has two strawlike tubes. One of these tubes is used by a mosquito to shoot saliva into a host, while the other is used to suck up the host's blood.

Puberty: Puberty is the time when a kid's body begins to change to become more adult. Some changes you can see, including the growth and development of breasts in girls, and facial hair in boys. A change in both sexes is an increase in sweat, which happens when apocrine sweat glands turn on in the genital areas and under the armpits.

Receptors or **sensors:** Receptors or sensors are cells that are specially designed to allow us to feel, taste, smell, hear, and see things. Some examples of receptors in the skin include pain receptors (we have them everywhere in the body, except inside the brain), touch receptors (we have them in our skin and in many of our organs), and smell receptors (*see smell receptors*).

Red blood cells: Red blood cells are tiny cells in our blood that are filled with the chemical hemoglobin. Hemoglobin transports oxygen in our blood and gives blood its red color.

Reflex: A reflex is the way your nervous system protects you by reacting quickly to something your body senses, without you having to think about it. If you touch a hot stove, for example, your nervous system senses heat and pain and causes you to *reflexively* jerk your finger away, before you even realize you've touched the stove. Wrinkling of the fingers is a reflex that slows blood flow to the fingers when a lot of water seeps in, to help your grip.

Sebaceous gland(s): The scientific name for oil glands. *See oil glands*

Shed: When things are shed, they come off. Dead skin cells are constantly shed from the very top of the epidermis, and they end up clinging to the inside of your clothes, floating off into the air, or getting left behind on all the things you touch.

Shivering: When you shiver, your muscles begin to shake by contracting and relaxing quickly.

When muscles contract, they also make heat, so shivering warms the body. When we get sick, shivering helps to create a fever that kills off germs.

Smell receptors: Smell receptors are nerve cells found deep in the back part of the nose, which can detect different smells in the air. They then carry information about these smells to the brain.

Sudoriferous glands: The scientific name for sweat glands. *See sweat glands*

Sulfur compounds: Sulfur compounds are any chemicals that contain sulfur. Some of these compounds have stinky odors and are found in foods like onion and garlic. When we eat these foods, we often release the smelly sulfur compounds in our sweat. Many other sulfur compounds, like those found in coal, gasoline, and penicillin, do not stink at all.

Sweat glands: Sweat glands (also called "sudoriferous glands") are packets of cells in skin that make sweat. They are found all over our skin. An adult has between two and five million sweat glands. Sweat cools our body, gets rid of some wastes, and helps our hands and feet grip objects.

Thermoregulate: Thermoregulate (thermoregulation) is the term for all the things our bodies do to keep our temperature at around a normal 98.7°F. Our skin makes sweat, which helps keep us from getting too warm, and has a layer of fat that keeps us from getting too cold. Our muscles keep us warm by making us shiver. Our blood vessels help as well; they can close up on the skin's surface to hold heat in, or open to let heat out.

Tissues: Tissues are groups of cells that work together to do particular jobs in the body. For example, the epidermis is a tissue in our skin that covers and protects, and the dermis is a tissue that provides nutrients and supports the epidermis. Different tissues come together to form all our different organs, like our bones, our skin, our stomach, and our heart.

UV, or **Ultraviolet**, **rays:** Ultraviolet radiation, or UV rays, is one form of invisible energy from sunlight that reaches the Earth. Though we can't see it, we can still feel it. UV rays can penetrate our skin and help us make vitamin D, but too much exposure to them can cause a dangerous suntan or sunburn.

Virus: A virus is a kind of invader that gets into a body's cells and uses the cells to make more viruses. Viruses are so tiny that they can only be seen using a powerful electron microscope. Different kinds of viruses cause different diseases. In addition to warts, viruses can cause colds, chicken pox, and measles.

Vitamin D: Vitamin D is a chemical that is important for the growth of bones. It is found in fish and eggs and can be added to milk. It is also made in our skin when we absorb certain UV rays from the sun.

White blood cells: There are many types of white blood cells in our blood. White blood cells are larger than red blood cells and look white under a microscope. They play an important role in fighting off infections.

Whiteheads: A whitehead forms when a hair follicle gets clogged with extra oil and dead skin cells. This mixture plugs up the follicle opening, or pore, and causes a swelling in the skin which looks like a white dot. The whitehead is covered by skin, and so it is not exposed to the air like a blackhead; oxygen in the air turns a blackhead black by breaking down the dead skin cells in the follicle. Without air, whiteheads stay white.

FOR MORE INFORMATION

Useful Websites

Animals changing colors: This article includes fascinating photos, videos, and information about animals that change colors: webecoist.momtastic.com/2009/02/22/color-changing-strange-animals-species

Healing skin: This informative article about skin includes wonderful moving images of skin and the process of skin healing: science.nationalgeographic.com/science/health-and-human-body/human-body/skin-article

Kidshealth.org: This website includes clear discussions of skin for kids and their parents. Some examples include:

Your Skin

kidshealth.org/kid/cancer_center/HTBW/skin.html

What's a Scab?

kidshealth.org/kid/talk/yucky/scab.html

Blisters, Calluses, and Corns

kidshealth.org/kid/ill_injure/aches/blisters.html#

Acne

kidshealth.org/en/kids/acne.html

What Are Freckles?

kidshealth.org/kid/talk/qa/freckles.html

What's Up with Warts?

kidshealth.org/kid/ill_injure/aches/warts.html

What's Sweat?

kidshealth.org/kid/talk/yucky/sweat.html

A Kid's Guide to Fever

kidshealth.org/en/kids.fever.html?ref=search&WT.ac=msh-k-dtop-en-search-clk

What's a Bruise?

kidshealth.org/kid/talk/qa/bruise.html

Sweat glands: These moving images show how sweat glands release sweat (to see them, you'll need Adobe Flash): mayoclinic.org/how-sweating-and-body-odor-occur/flh-20078307

WebMD: This website includes lots of additional information about skin issues covered in the book. Some examples include:

Blisters

webmd.com/skin-problems-and-treatments/tc/blisters-topic-overview

Warts

webmd.com/skin-problems-and-treatments/warts-faq-questions-answers

Poison Ivy, Oak, or Sumac

webmd.com/allergies/tc/poison-ivy-oak-or-sumac-topic-overview

References and Additional Reading

"About Mosquitoes." Mosquito World. (nd). Accessed September 3, 2012. mosquitoworld.net/aboutmosquitoes.php.

Adelman, Steven, C. Richard Taylor, and Norman C. Heglund. "Sweating on Paws and Palms: What Is Its Function?" *American Journal of Physiology—Legacy Content* vol. 229, no. 5 (1975): 1,400–02.

Allbrook, David. "The Morphology of the Subdermal Glands of *Hippopotamus Amphibius*." *Journal of Zoology* vol. 139, no. 1 (1962): 67–73.

Baudinette, R. V., J. P. Loveridge, K. J. Wilson, C. D. Mills, and K. Schmidt-Nielsen. "Heat Loss from Feet of Herring Gulls at Rest and During Flight." *American Journal of Physics* vol. 230, no. 4 (1976): 920–24.

Bauernfeind, Robert J., Randall A. Higgins, and Lowell Breeden. "Blister Beetles in Alfalfa." Kansas State University Agricultural Experiment Station and Cooperative Extension Service. (1990). Accessed February 14, 2013. bookstore.ksre.ksu.edu/pubs/mf959.pdf.

Bernerd Françoise, Claire Marionnet, and Christine Duval. "Solar Ultraviolet Radiation Induces Biological Alterations in Human Skin In Vitro: Relevance of a Well-Balanced UVA/UVB Protection." *Indian Journal of Dermatology, Venereology, and Leprology* vol. 78, no. 7 (2012): 15–23.

"Blisters—Home Treatment." WebMD. (nd). Accessed February 14, 2013. webmd.com/skin-problems-and-treatments/tc/blisters-home-treatment.

Brass, Lawrence. "Understanding and Evaluating Platelet Function." In *Hematology 2010* vol. 8, no. 5. American Society of Hematology. (2010): 387–96.

Chanda, Silpi, Shalini Kushwaha, and Raj Kumar Tiwari. "Garlic as Food, Spice and Medicine: A Perspective." *Journal of Pharmacy Research* vol. 4, no. 6 (2011): 1,857–60.

Changizi, Mark, Romann Weber, Ritesh Kotecha, and Joseph Palazzo. "Are Wet-Induced Wrinkled Fingers Primate Rain Treads?" *Brain, Behavior and Evolution* vol. 77, no. 4 (2011): 286–90.

Chapman, David M., and Uldis Roze. "Functional Histology of Quill Erection in the Porcupine, Erethizon Dorsatum." *Canadian Journal of Zoology* vol. 75, no. 1 (1997): 1–10.

Clydesdale, Gavin J., Geoffrey W. Dandie, and H. Konrad Muller. "Ultraviolet Light Induced Injury: Immunological and Inflammatory Effects." *Immunology and Cell Biology* vol. 79, no. 6 (2001.): 547–68. doi:10.1046/j.1440-1711.2001.01047.x.

Cole, G. W. "Australian School Innovation in Science, Mathematics Forensic Investigations. Fingerprinting, Teacher Background Information," staff.katyisd.org/sites/1301084/Documents/About%20Forensics.pdf. Accessed March 29, 2018.

———. "Freckles." MedicineNet. (August 2017). Accessed January 28, 2013. medicinenet.com/freckles/article.htm#freckles_facts.

Costin, Gertrude-E., and Vincent J. Hearing. "Human Skin Pigmentation: Melanocytes Modulate Skin Color in Response to Stress." *The FASEB Journal* vol. 21, no. 4 (2007.): 976–94.

Crew, Bec. "New Skin-Feeding Amphibian Found in French Guiana." Scientific American. (2013.) Accessed February 14, 2013. blogs.scientificamerican.com/running-ponies/2013/04/17/new-skin-feeding-amphibian-found-in-french-guiana.

Demain, Jeffrey G. "Papular Urticaria and Things That Bite in the Night." *Current Allergy and Asthma Reports* vol. 3, no. 4 (2003): 291–303.

Fabacher, David. L., and Edward E. Little. "Skin Component May Protect Fishes from Ultraviolet-B Radiation." *Environmental Science and Pollution Research.* Vol. 2, no. 1 (1995): 30–32.

French, Mike, and Brian Yamashita. "Latent Print Development." In *The Fingerprint Sourcebook.* US Department of Justice. Rockville, MD: National Institute of Justice/NCJRS, 2011.

Guo, Shujuan, and Luisa A. DiPietro. "Factors Affecting Wound Healing." *Journal of Dental Research* vol. 89, no. 3 (2010): 219–29.

Hashimoto, Kimiko, Yoko Saikawa, and Masaya Nakata. "Studies on the Red Sweat of the Hippopotamus Amphibius." *Pure and Applied Chemistry* vol. 79, no. 4 (2007): 507–17.

Heidt, Gary A., and Leland F. Morgans. "Comparative Histology of the Scent Glands of Five Species of Skunks." *Journal of Anatomy* vol. 134, pt. 1 (1982): 121.

Hidden, Philippa Ann. "Thermoregulation in African Elephants (*Loxodonta Africana*)." MS diss., University of the Witwatersrand, 2009.

Holick, Michael F. "Sunlight, UV-Radiation, Vitamin D and Skin Cancer: How Much Sunlight Do We Need?" In *Sunlight, Vitamin D and Skin Cancer: Advances in Experimental Medicine and Biology.* Jörg Reichrath (ed.). New York: Springer Science & Business Media LLC., 2008: 1–15.

Hughes, V. K., P. S. Ellis, T. Burt, and N. E. I. Langlois. "The Practical Application of Reflectance Spectrophotometry for the Demonstration of Haemoglobin and its Degradation in Bruises." *Journal of Clinical Pathology* vol. 57, no.4 (2004): 355–59.

Ingram, D. L. "Evaporative Cooling in the Pig." *Nature* vol. 207 (1965): 415–16.

——. "Stimulation of Cutaneous Glands in the Pig." *Journal of Comparative Pathology* vol. 77, no.1 (1967): 93–98.

Jabr, Ferris. "What the Supercool Arctic Ground Squirrel Teaches Us About the Brain's Resilience." Scientific American. (2012). Accessed February 3, 2014. scientificamerican.com/article/arctic-ground-squirrel-brain.

Jain, Anil K., Salil Prabhakar, and Sharath Pankanti. "On the Similarity of Identical Twin Fingerprints." *Pattern Recognition* vol. 35, no. 11 (2002): 2,653–63.

Jappe, Uta. "Pathological Mechanisms of Acne with Special Emphasis on Propionibacterium Acnes and Related Therapy." *Acta Dermato Venereologica* vol. 83, no. 4 (2003).

Kang, W. "How Do Squid and Octopuses Change Color?" *Scientific American* vol. 284, no. 5 (2001): 100.

Kligman, Albert M. "An Overview of Acne." *Journal of Investigative Dermatology* vol. 62, no. 3 (1974): 268–87.

Knapik, Joseph J., Katy L. Reynolds, Kathryn L. Duplantis, and Bruce H. Jones. "Friction Blisters." *Sports Medicine* vol., 20, no. 3 (1995): 136–47.

Kong, X. Q., and C. W. Wu. "Mosquito Proboscis: An Elegant Biomicroelectromechanical System." *Physical Review E* vol. 82, no. 1 (2010): 11,910.

Langlois, N.E.I., and G. A. Gresham. "The Ageing of Bruises: A Review and Study of the Colour Changes with Time." *Forensic Science International* vol. 50, no. 2 (1991): 227–38.

Larue, Jennifer Huget. "Will Nothing Stop That Infernal Itch?" *Washington Post.* (July 31, 2007). Accessed September 3, 2012. washingtonpost.com/wp-dyn/content/article/2007/07/27/AR2007072702155.html.

Lowe, N. J. "An Overview of Ultraviolet Radiation, Sunscreens, and Photo-Induced Dermatoses." *Dermatol Clinics* vol. 24, no. 1 (2006.): 9–17.

Mahmoud, B. H., C. L. Hexsel, I. H. Hamzavi, and H. W. Lim. "Effects of Visible Light on the Skin." *Photochemistry and Photobiology* vol. 84, no. 2 (2008): 450–62.

Martini, Frederic H., William C. Ober, Edwin F. Bartholomew, and Judi L. Nath. *Essentials of Anatomy and Physiology.* Boston: Pearson Education, 2012.

"Melanin, Melanocytes, and Melanosomes." Palaeobiology Research Group. (nd). Accessed October 9, 2012. palaeo.gly.bris.ac.uk/Melanosomes/melanin.html.

Milius, Susan. "Red Sweat: Hippo Skin Oozes Antibiotic Sunscreen." Science News. (2004). Accessed February 21, 2013. sciencenews.org/article/red-sweat-hippo-skin-oozes-antibiotic-sunscreen.

Montagna, William, Giuseppe Prota, and John A. Kenney Jr. *Black Skin: Structure and Function.* Cambridge, MA: Academic Press, 1993.

Montagu, Ashley. *Touching: The Human Significance of the Skin.* 3rd edition. New York: William Morrow Paperbacks, 1986.

"Mosquito Biology and Behavior. A Teacher's Resource Guide." Compiled by Marc Seligson. (Fall 2010). Accessed February 3, 2014. blogs.cornell.edu/naturalistoutreach/files/2013/09/Mosquitos-1715p2s.pdf.

"Mosquitoes." District, Greater Los Angeles County Vector Control. (2012–2016). Accessed September 3, 2012. glacvcd.org/vector-information/mosquitoes.

Nasr, Christian. "Flushing." Cleveland Clinic Center for Continuing Education. (2012). Accessed March 12, 2013. clevelandclinicmeded.com/medicalpubs/diseasemanagement/endocrinology/flushing.

Norman, M. D., J. Finn, and T. Tregenza. "Dynamic Mimicry in an Indo-Malayan Octopus." In *Proceedings of the Royal Society B* vol. 268, no. 1,478. London: Royal Society, 2001: 1,755–58.

Patel, E. K., A. Gupta, and R. J. Oswal. "A Review On: Mosquito Repellent Methods." In *International Journal of Pharmaceutical, Chemical and Biological Sciences* vol. 2, no. 3 (2012): 310–317.

Pinney, Roy. *The Snake Book*. New York: Doubleday, 1981.

Polefka, T. G., T. A. Meyer, P. P. Agin, and R. J. Bianchini. "Effects of Solar Radiation on the Skin." *Journal of Cosmetic Dermatology* vol. 11, no. 2 (2012): 134–43.

Rees, Jonathan L. "Genetics of Hair and Skin Color." *Annual Review of Genetics*. Vol. 37. (2003): 67–90.

Reunala, Timo, Henrikki Brummer-Korvenkontio, and Timo Palosuo. "Are We Really Allergic to Mosquito Bites?" *Annals of Medicine* vol. 26, no. 4 (1994): 301–306.

Saikawa, Yoko, Kimiko Hashimoto, Masaya Nakata, Masato Yoshihara, Kiyoshi Nagai, Motoyasu Ida, and Teruyuki Komiya. "Pigment Chemistry: The Red Sweat of the Hippopotamus." *Nature* vol. 429 (2004): 363.

Saladin, Kenneth S. *Anatomy & Physiology: The Unity of Form and Function*. 5th edition. New York: McGraw-Hill, 2010.

Shiel Jr., William C. "What Are Symptoms and Signs of a Bruise, and Why Does It Change Color?" In "Bumps & Bruises (Contusions and Ecchymoses)." Medicinenet. (nd). Accessed September 12, 2012. medicinenet.com/bruises/index.htm.

Siju, K. P., and Rickard Ignell. "Neuromodulation in the Chemosensory System of Mosquitoes—Neuroanatomy and Physiology." (2009).

Silverberg, Nanette B. "Human papillomavirus Infections in Children." In *Pediatric Infectious Diseases Revisited*. H. Schroten and S. Wirth (eds.). Birkhäuser Advances in Infectious Diseases. Germany: Springer, 2007: 365–90.

Smallegange, Renate C., Niels O. Verhulst, and Willem Takken. "Sweaty Skin: An Invitation to Bite?" *Trends in Parasitology* vol. 27, no. 4 (2011): 143–48.

Somnathe, Nitin D., Mahendra D. Kshirsagar, and Pravin K. Bhoyar. "An Overview on a Special Emphasis on Acne with Remedies." World Journal of Pharmacy and Pharmaceutical Sciences. (2012). Accessed January 14, 2013.

Stuart-Fox, Devi, and Adnan Moussalli. "Camouflage in Colour-Changing Animals." In *Animal Camouflage: Mechanisms and Function*. Martin Stevens and Sami Merilaita (eds). Cambridge, UK: Cambridge University Press, 2011: 237.

———. "Camouflage, Communication and Thermoregulation: Lessons from Colour Changing Organisms." *Philosophical Transactions of the Royal Society B* vol. 364, no. 1,516 (2009): 463–70.

Sudhakar, G. K., Vasudev Pai, Arvind Pai, and Venkatesh Kamath. "Therapeutic Approaches in the Management of Plantar Warts by Human Papillomaviruses: A Review." *Asian Journal of Biomedical and Pharmaceutical Sciences*. Vol. 3, no. 26. (2013): 1.

Théry Marc, and Jérôme Casas. "The Multiple Disguises of Spiders: Web Colour and Decorations, Body Colour And Movement." *Philosophical Transactions of the Royal Society B* vol. 364, no. 1,516 (2009): 471–80.

"Understanding Plantar Warts—The Basics." WebMD. (nd). Accessed February 26, 2014. webmd.com/skin-problems-and-treatments/tc/warts-and-plantar-warts-topic-overview.

Van Laethem, A., S. Claerhout, M. Garmyn, and P. Agostinis. "The Sunburn Cell: Regulation of Death and Survival of the Keratinocyte." *International Journal of Biochemistry and Cell Biology* vol. 37, no. 8. (2005): 1,547–53.

Well, Danielle. "Acne Vulgaris: A Review of Causes and Treatment Options." *The Nurse Practitioner* vol. 38, no.10 (2013): 22–31.

Wiese, Jim. *Head to Toe Science: Over 40 Eye-Popping, Spine-Tingling, Heart-Pounding Activities That Teach Kids about the Human Body.* New York: Wiley, 2000.

Wilder-Smith, Einar P. V., and Adeline Chow. "Water-Immersion Wrinkling Is Due to Vasoconstriction." *Muscle & Nerve* vol. 27, no. 3 (2003): 307–11.

Wilke, K., A. Martin, L. Terstegen, and S. S. Biel. "A Short History of Sweat Gland Biology." *International Journal of Cosmetic Science* vol. 29, no. 3 (2007): 169–79.

World Health Organization. World Meteorological Organization, United Nations Environment Programme, and International Commission on Non-Ionizing Radiation Protection. "Global Solar UV Index: A Practical Guide." (2002). Accessed February 12, 2013. who.int/uv/publications/en/GlobalUVI.pdf.

Yamashita, Brian, R. V. Baudinette, J. P. Loveridge, K. J. Wilson, C. D. Mills, K. Schmidt-Nielsen. Fingerprinting, Teacher Background Information. Australian School Innovation in Science, Mathematics Forensic Investigations. (1976). Accessed December 19, 2012. clt.uwa.edu.au/__data/page/112506/fsp07_fingerprinting.pdf.

Yamaguchi, Yuji, Michaela Brenner, and Vincent J. Hearing. "The Regulation of Skin Pigmentation." *The Journal of Biological Chemistry* vol. 282, no. 38 (2007): 27,557–61.

Zamzow, Jill P., and George S. Losey. "Ultraviolet Radiation Absorbance by Coral Reef Fish Mucus: Photo-Protection and Visual Communication." *Environmental Biology of Fishes* vol. 63, no. 1 (2002): 41–47.

Zwiebel, L. J., and W. Takken. "Olfactory Regulation of Mosquito–Host Interactions." *Insect Biochemistry and Molecular Biology* vol. 34, no. 7 (2004): 645–52.

INDEX

adrenaline, 21, 77

ammonia, 40, 51, 77

AMS (allyl methyl sulfide), 40

antiseptic, 70, 77

anuses, 40, 77

apocrine sweat glands, 40, 77

arrector pili, 31–34, 77

bacteria

    animal sweat and, 17

    contagious, 77, 78

    raw meat and, 8

    smelly sweat and, 39

bilirubin, 46–47, 77

biliverdin, 46–47, 77

blackheads, 65–67, 77

blisters, 64, 69–71, 75, 81

blood cells

    red, 48–49, 77, 79

    white, 54, 57, 78, 80

blushing, 21

bruise, 41, 45–47

caecilians, 3

camouflage, 13

cantharidin, 71

capillary(ies), 5, 42, 45, 54, 56, 72, 77

carotene, 11–12, 77, 79

cell division, 4, 77

clots, blood, 43–44, 49, 54, 77, 78

clotting process, 43–44, 49, 77

CO₂, 51, 77

collagen, 5, 77

colors, skin (See skin colors)

contagious viruses/bacteria, 72, 77

cut skin, 41–44, 49, 72, 77

dermis (dermal regions), 4–8, 35–36, 77, 78, 80

diffuse, 6, 77–78

epidermis

    about, 4, 7, 77–79

    shedding, 4–5, 28, 59, 78, 80

    viruses in, 72

evaporation, 36, 78

fibrin threads, 43, 77, 78

fingerprints, 24–27

follicle(s), 6, 77–80

freckles, 18–20

genes, 11, 18, 78

goose bumps, 24, 31–33

hemocyanin, 48

hemoglobin, 11, 45–48, 77–79

hemosiderin, 46–47, 77

hibernation, 53, 63

histamine, 54–55, 78

hormones, 67, 77

HPV, 72, 78

hypodermis, 7–8, 78

hypothalamus, 62, 78

immunity, 73, 78

inflammation, 56, 78

infrared radiation, 56, 78

ink stains on fingers, 28

itchy skin, 50–55

kinins, 57, 78

lactic acid, 40, 51, 78

layers of skin, 4–10, 28, 54, 60, 78

melanin

    about, 10–12, 79

    blackheads and, 67

    freckles and, 18

    skin color and, 10–12

    suntans/sunburns and, 14, 16

melanocytes, 10–12, 79

mosquitoes, 40, 44, 51–55, 77

nutrient(s), 2, 6, 53, 77, 79–80

oil glands (sebaceous glands), 5–6, 65–67, 77–79

organ, 3, 78–80

oxygen, 3, 6, 45, 48, 77–79

pain receptors, 6, 57, 78–79

panting, 37

peeling skin, 59–60

pigment, 11, 77, 79

pimples, 64–68, 75, 77–78

plasma, 54, 79

platelet plug, 43, 79

platelets, 42, 77, 79

pore(s), 67, 79–80

proboscis, 54, 79

puberty, 38, 68, 79

receptors

    about, 6, 79

    pain, 6, 57, 78–79

    smell, 39–40, 79–80

    touch, 2, 6, 79–80

red, skin turning, 9, 14–16, 21, 45, 56–57

red blood cells, 48–49, 77, 79

reflex, 29, 79

scabs, 41, 49, 75, 81

sebaceous glands (*See* oil glands)

sensors, 6, 79

shades of skin colors (*See* skin colors)

shedding skin cells, 4–5, 28, 59–60, 79

shivering, 31, 62, 78–80

skin, basic facts about, 2–3

skin-breathing animals, 3

skin colors

    about, 9–13, 18

    UV rays and, 14–17

smell receptors, 39–40, 79–80

sudoriferous glands (*See* sweat glands)

sulfur compounds, 40, 80

sunburns, 14–17, 56–59, 78, 80

sunscreen, 15–18, 57–58, 75

suntans, 14–18, 80

sweat glands (sudoriferous glands), 6, 35–40, 51, 80

tail prints, 27

temperatures, 2, 61–63, 78–80

thermoregulate, 2, 80

tissues, 77–80

touch receptors, 2, 6, 79–80

ultraviolet rays (*See* UV rays)

UV rays, 2, 14–17, 56, 80

viruses, 72, 77–78, 80

vitamin D, 2, 80

warm, keeping, 2, 13, 22–23, 33, 62, 78, 80

warts, 72–74, 77–78, 80–81

washing hands, 8

white, fingers turning white, 22

white blood cells, 54, 57, 78, 80

whiteheads, 65–67, 80

wrinkled skin, 29–30